INDIANA POST OFFICE MURAL GUIDEBOOK

DAVID W. GATES JR.

POST OFFICE FANS
Crystal Lake, Illinois

Post Office Fans
PO Box 11
Crystal Lake, IL 60039
Phone: 815-206-8405
info@postofficefans.com • www.postofficefans.com

Cover and text design by John Reinhardt Book Design
Cover photo: Spencer Post Office, Spencer, Indiana
Angola Indiana photo courtesy of the Carnegie Public Library of Steuben County

CONTENTS

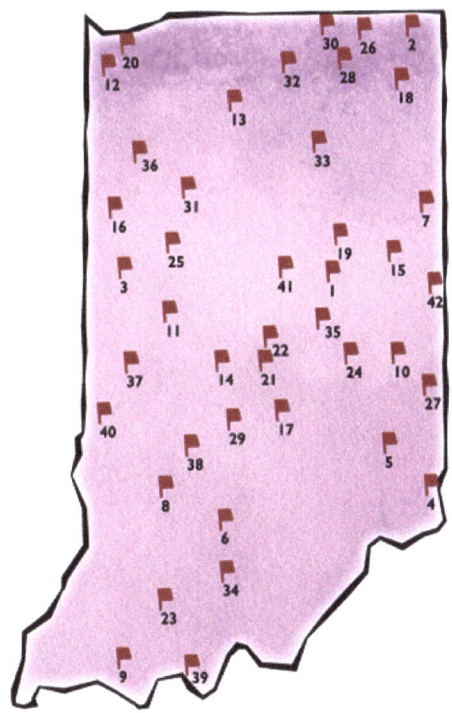

PREFACE

THE STATISTICS I'VE READ report there are somewhere between 1,100 and 1,400 works of art located in public post offices nationwide. Since I've been unable to verify these statistics, I've made it my mission to find out exactly how many exist and view them all.

What began for me as a casual interest in a photographic subject soon became a deep fascination with the history and presence of a unique moment in American culture and art. Before creating this guidebook, I visited hundreds of post offices and spoke to dozens of people across the U.S., and I realized we were united in our enthusiasm for keeping the stories of this art alive and available for the American public.

The guidebook you are viewing today is an account of all 42 of Indiana's New Deal post office murals. I encourage you to visit one of these post offices in Indiana or seek out one in your own state. To learn about this special art is to learn about the continuing American journey.

Our guidebooks continue to be a great resource for post office enthusiasts. Since I'm from Illinois, I found it fitting to create one for our neighbor state—Indiana. This led to the book you are holding today. It provides a quick reference to the Depression-era post office murals in Indiana.

There are no images of the murals in this book. It is meant solely as a reference for the buildings and towns in Indiana. This guide provides: full address, title of the artwork, artist, medium and status. I've found having a book like this makes for a handy reference and personal checklist while traveling around the state.

I've created this guidebook for your benefit, in case you find yourself needing the same checklist as you travel and discover each building and mural. I hope this book brings you enjoyment and knowledge. There is no need to scour multiple sources to find the status of each one. I've done the work for you. Print it out or download it to your mobile device to bring with you on your next post office visit.

Thank you,

David W. Gates Jr.

INTRODUCTION

FROM 1934–1943, fascinating murals and various forms of art were commissioned and installed in public buildings under the United States Treasury Department's Section of Painting and Sculpture, later renamed the Section of Fine Arts.

My research revealed two reasons for installing art in post offices. The first was to bring light and hope to a country gripped by the Great Depression, and the second was to employ artists during this difficult time.

Anonymous competitions were held to select artists for new federal buildings that were being constructed during this time. Commissions paid to the artists were approximately one percent of the congressional appropriation to construct the new post office buildings.

This informative book lists all the post offices in Indiana that received artwork. It gives you a quick reference to the New Deal post office murals in Indiana. It includes:

- Full address
- Artist
- Title
- Medium
- Status
- Link for further reading

While this guide does not provide images of the actual art, it does provide a quick reference to the post office art in Indiana. Although the title of the book says "mural," I use that term inclusively. Indiana is lucky to have also received art commissioned in other mediums such as terra-cotta, stone, wood and limestone.

ALEXANDRIA

ADDRESS: 205 W. Church St., Alexandria, Indiana 46001

ARTIST: Roland Schweinsburg

TITLE: *The Sleighing Party*

MEDIUM: Oil on canvas (mural)

STATUS: The Alexandria post office is still an active, operating facility, and the mural can be viewed by interested members of the public. It resides in the lobby on the wall above the postmaster's door.

WEB: www.postofficefans.com/alexandria-indiana-post-office/

ANGOLA

ADDRESS: 200 E. Maumee St., Angola, Indiana 46703

ARTIST: Charles Campbell

TITLE: *Hoosier Farm*

MEDIUM: Oil on canvas (mural)

STATUS: The former Angola post office, depicted here, was razed years ago. The mural was relocated to the Steuben County Community Center on Wayne Street. Interested parties should call ahead for hours and accessibility. It is located on the second floor of the building.

WEB: www.postofficefans.com/angola-indiana-former-post-office/

ATTICA

ADDRESS: 107 E. Main St., Attica, Indiana 47918

ARTIST: Reva Jackman

TITLE: *Trek of the Covered Wagon to Indiana*

MEDIUM: Oil on canvas (mural)

STATUS: The Attica post office is still an active, operating facility, and the mural can be viewed by interested members of the public. It resides in the lobby on the wall above the postmaster's door.

WEB: www.postofficefans.com/attica-indiana-post-office/

Aurora

ADDRESS: 501 3rd St., Aurora, Indiana, 47001

ARTIST: Henrik Martin Mayer

TITLE: *Down to the Ferry*

MEDIUM: Oil on canvas (mural)

STATUS: The Aurora post office is still an active, operating facility, and the mural can be viewed by interested members of the public. It resides in the lobby on the wall above the postmaster's door.

WEB: www.postofficefans.com/aurora-indiana-post-office/

BATESVILLE

ADDRESS: 3 W. George St., Batesville, Indiana 47006

ARTIST: Orville Carroll

TITLE: *Building the Industrial Foundations of Batesville*

MEDIUM: Tempera on canvas (mural)

STATUS: The Batesville post office is still an active, operating facility, and the mural can be viewed by interested members of the public. It resides in the lobby on the wall above the postmaster's door.

WEB: www.postofficefans.com/batesville-indiana-post-office/

BEDFORD

ADDRESS: 1324 K St., Bedford, Indiana 47421

ARTIST: John Fabion

TITLE: *Limestone Quarry Workers*

MEDIUM: Terra-cotta (relief)

STATUS: The former Bedford post office is no longer an active, operating postal facility. The relief was moved to the newer building on H Street. It resides on a wall in the retail section of the lobby. It is best viewed during business hours.

WEB: www.postofficefans.com/bedford-indiana-former-post-office/

BERNE

ADDRESS: 215 W. Main St., Berne, Indiana 46711

ARTIST: Walter Gardner

TITLE: *Christmas Morning Mail*

MEDIUM: Oil on canvas (mural)

STATUS: The Berne post office is still an active, operating facility. However, the mural is missing, lost, or destroyed. It formerly resided here in the lobby on the wall above the postmaster's door.

WEB: www.postofficefans.com/berne-indiana-post-office/

BLOOMFIELD

ADDRESS: 55 N. Washington St., Bloomfield, Indiana 47424

ARTIST: Lilian Swann Saarinen

TITLE: *Waiting for the Mail*

MEDIUM: Terra-cotta (relief)

STATUS: The Bloomfield post office is still an active, operating facility, and the relief can be viewed by interested members of the public. It resides in the retail section of the lobby on the wall above the postmaster's door. It is best viewed during business hours.

WEB: www.postofficefans.com/bloomfield-indiana-post-office/

BOONVILLE

ADDRESS: 214 W. Locust St., Boonville, Indiana 47601

ARTIST: Ida Abelman

TITLE: *Boonville Beginnings*

MEDIUM: Tempera (mural)

STATUS: The Boonville post office is still an active, operating facility, and the mural can be viewed by interested members of the public. It resides in the lobby on the wall above the postmaster's door.

WEB: www.postofficefans.com/boonville-indiana-post-office/

CAMBRIDGE CITY

ADDRESS: 227 W. Main St., Cambridge City, Indiana 47327

ARTIST: Samuel Franklin Hershey

TITLE: *Pride of Cambridge City*

MEDIUM: Oil on canvas (mural)

STATUS: The Cambridge City post office is still an active, operating facility, and the mural can be viewed by interested members of the public. It resides in the lobby on the wall above the postmaster's door.

WEB: www.postofficefans.com/cambridge-city-indiana-post-office/

CRAWFORDSVILLE

ADDRESS: 300 E. Main St., Crawfordsville, Indiana 47933

ARTIST: Frank Long

TITLE: *Indiana Agriculture*

MEDIUM: Oil on canvas (mural)

STATUS: The Crawfordsville post office is still an active, operating facility, and the mural can be viewed by interested members of the public. It resides in the lobby on the wall above the postmaster's door.

WEB: www.postofficefans.com/crawfordsville-indiana-post-office/

CROWN POINT

ADDRESS: 128 S. East St., Crown Point, Indiana 46307

ARTIST: George Melville Smith

TITLE: *From Such Beginnings Sprang the County of Lake*

MEDIUM: Oil on canvas (mural)

STATUS: The Crown Point post office is still an active, operating facility, and the mural can be viewed by interested members of the public. It resides in the lobby on the wall above the postmaster's door.

WEB: www.postofficefans.com/crown-point-indiana-post-office/

CULVER

ADDRESS: 115 W. Jefferson St., Culver, Indiana 46511

ARTIST: Jessie Hull Mayer

TITLE: *The Arrival of the Mail in Culver*

MEDIUM: Oil on canvas (mural)

STATUS: The Culver post office is still an active, operating facility, and the mural can be viewed by interested members of the public. It resides in the lobby on the wall above the postmaster's door.

WEB: www.postofficefans.com/culver-indiana-post-office/

DANVILLE

ADDRESS: 101 W. Marion St., Danville, Indiana 46122

ARTIST: Gail Wycoff Martin

TITLE: *Filling the Water Jugs–Haymaking Time*

MEDIUM: Oil on canvas (mural)

STATUS: The former Danville post office is no longer an active post-al facility. However, the mural still resides in the building. Interested members of the public should contact the Hendricks County probation office for hours and accessibility. It resides in the former lobby on the wall above what was once the postmaster's door.

WEB: www.postofficefans.com/danville-indiana-former-post-office/

DUNKIRK

ADDRESS: 123 W. Commerce St., Dunkirk, Indiana 47336

ARTIST: Frances Foy

TITLE: *Preparations for Dunkirk Autumn Festival*

MEDIUM: Oil on canvas (mural)

STATUS: The Dunkirk post office is still an active, operating facility, and the mural can be viewed by interested members of the public. It resides in the lobby on the wall above the postmaster's door.

WEB: www.postofficefans.com/dunkirk-indiana-post-office/

FOWLER

ADDRESS: 114 S. Madison Ave., Fowler, Indiana 47944

ARTIST: Nat Werner

TITLE: *Rest during Prairie Plowing*

MEDIUM: Cast stone (relief)

STATUS: The Fowler post office is still an active, operating facility, and the relief can be viewed by interested members of the public. It resides in the lobby on the wall above the postmaster's door.

WEB: www.postofficefans.com/fowler-indiana-post-office/

FRANKLIN

ADDRESS: 55 W. Madison Street, Franklin, Indiana 46131

ARTIST: Jean Swiggett

TITLE: *Local Industry*

MEDIUM: Oil on canvas (mural)

STATUS: The former Franklin post office is no longer an active, operating postal facility. It is now home to the RFD Franklin Restaurant. The mural was moved to the newer building on Main Street, and can be viewed by interested members of the public. It resides in the lobby, on a wall above the post office boxes.

WEB: www.postofficefans.com/franklin-indiana-former-post-office/

GARRETT

ADDRESS: 115 W. Keyser St., Garrett, Indiana 46738

ARTIST: Joseph H. Cox

TITLE: *Clearing the Right of Way*

MEDIUM: Oil on canvas (mural)

STATUS: The Garrett post office is still an active, operating facility, and the mural can be viewed by interested members of the public. It resides in the lobby on the wall above the postmaster's door.

WEB: www.postofficefans.com/garrett-indiana-post-office/

GAS CITY

ADDRESS: 123 N. 2nd St., Gas City, Indiana 46933

ARTIST: William Adelbert Dolwick

TITLE: *Gas City in Boom Days*

MEDIUM: Oil on canvas (mural)

STATUS: The Gas City post office is still an active, operating facility, and the mural can be viewed by interested members of the public. It resides in the lobby on the wall above the postmaster's door.

WEB: www.postofficefans.com/gas-city-indiana-post-office/

HOBART

ADDRESS: 221 Main St., Hobart, Indiana 46342

ARTIST: William Adelbert Dolwick

TITLE: *Early Hobart*

MEDIUM: Oil on canvas (mural)

STATUS: The Hobart post office is still an active, operating facility, and the mural can be viewed by interested members of the public. It resides in the lobby on the wall above the postmaster's door.

WEB: www.postofficefans.com/hobart-indiana-post-office/

INDIANAPOLIS– BIRCH BAYH

ADDRESS: 46 E. Ohio St., Indianapolis, Indiana 46204

ARTIST: Grant Christian and Reynolds Selfridge

TITLE: *Mail, Transportation and Delivery* and *Early and Present Day Indianapolis Life*

MEDIUM: Oil on canvas (murals) 9 panels

STATUS: The former downtown Indianapolis post office is no longer an active, operating postal facility. It is known as the Birch Bayh Federal Building. The murals reside in a hallway on the third floor. Interested parties should contact the local General Service Administration (GSA) office for hours and accessibility.

WEB: www.postofficefans.com/indianapolis-post-office-and-courthouse-birch-bayh-federal-building/

INDIANAPOLIS–
BIRCH BAYH (CONT'D)

ADDRESS: 46 E. Ohio St., Indianapolis, Indiana 46204

ARTIST: David Kresz Rubins

TITLE: *Distribution of the Mail*

MEDIUM: Limestone (reliefs)

STATUS: The former downtown Indianapolis post office is no longer an active, operating postal facility. It is known as the Birch Bayh Federal Building. The reliefs reside above the two garage entrances of the building. They are easily viewable from the sidewalk.

WEB: www.postofficefans.com/indianapolis-post-office-and-courthouse-birch-bayh-federal-building/

INDIANAPOLIS– BROAD RIPPLE

ADDRESS: 6255 Carrollton Ave., Broad Ripple, Indiana 46220

ARTIST: Alan Tompkins

TITLE: *Suburban Street*

MEDIUM: Oil on canvas (mural)

STATUS: The Indianapolis Broad Ripple post office is still an active, operating facility, and the mural can be viewed by interested members of the public. It resides on a wall in the main lobby.

WEB: www.postofficefans.com/indianapolis-indiana-post-office-broad-ripple-station/

JASPER

ADDRESS: 206 E. 6th St., Jasper, Indiana 47546

ARTIST: Jessie Hull Mayer

TITLE: *Indiana Farming Scene in Late Autumn*

MEDIUM: Oil on canvas (mural)

STATUS: The Jasper post office is still an active, operating facility, and the mural can be viewed by interested members of the public. It resides in the lobby on the wall above the postmaster's door.

WEB: www.postofficefans.com/jasper-indiana-post-office/

KNIGHTSTOWN

ADDRESS: 37 N. Jefferson St., Knightstown, Indiana 46148

ARTIST: Raymond L. Morris

TITLE: *The Evening Mail*

MEDIUM: Oil on canvas (mural)

STATUS: The Knightstown post office is still an active, operating facility, and the mural can be viewed by interested members of the public. It resides in the lobby on the wall above the postmaster's door.

WEB: www.postofficefans.com/knightstown-indiana-post-office/

LAFAYETTE

ADDRESS: 230 N. 4th St. Side, Lafayette, Indiana 47901

TITLE: *Rural Delivery* and *Sad News*

MEDIUM: Oil on canvas (murals)

STATUS: The Lafayette post office is still an active, operating facility, and the murals can be viewed by interested members of the public. They reside on a wall in the main lobby.

WEB: www.postofficefans.com/lafayette-downtown-station-indiana-post-office/

LaGrange

ADDRESS: 300 S. Detroit St., LaGrange, Indiana 46761

ARTIST: Jessie Hull Mayer

TITLE: *Corn School*

MEDIUM: Oil on canvas (mural)

STATUS: The LaGrange post office is still an active, operating facility, and the mural can be viewed by interested members of the public. It resides in the lobby on a wall above the postmaster's door.

WEB: www.postofficefans.com/lagrange-indiana-post-office/

LIBERTY

ADDRESS: 29 E. Union St., Liberty, Indiana 47353

ARTIST: Avery Johnson

TITLE: *Autumn Fields*

MEDIUM: Oil on canvas (mural)

STATUS: The Liberty post office is still an active, operating facility, and the mural can be viewed by interested members of the public. It resides in the lobby on the wall above the postmaster's door.

WEB: www.postofficefans.com/liberty-indiana-post-office/

LIGONIER

ADDRESS: 201 S. Main St., Ligonier, Indiana 46767

ARTIST: Fay Elizabeth Davis

TITLE: *Cutting Timber*

MEDIUM: Oil on canvas (mural)

STATUS: The Ligonier post office is still an active, operating facility, and the mural can be viewed by interested members of the public. It resides in the lobby on the wall above the postmaster's door.

WEB: www.postofficefans.com/ligonier-indiana-post-office/

MARTINSVILLE

ADDRESS: 10 S. Main St., Martinsville, Indiana 46151

ARTIST: Alan Tompkins

TITLE: *The Arrival of the Mail*

MEDIUM: Oil on canvas (mural)

STATUS: The Martinsville post office is still an active, operating facility, and the mural can be viewed by interested members of the public. It resides in the lobby on the wall above the postmaster's door.

WEB: www.postofficefans.com/martinsville-indiana-post-office/

MIDDLEBURY

ADDRESS: 200 S. Main St., Middlebury, Indiana 46540

ARTIST: Raymond Redell

TITLE: *Early Middlebury Mail*

MEDIUM: Oil on canvas (mural)

STATUS: The Middlebury post office is still an active, operating facility, and the mural can be viewed by interested members of the public. It resides in the lobby on the wall above the postmaster's door. It is best viewed during business hours when the retail section is open.

WEB: www.postofficefans.com/middlebury-indiana-post-office/

MONTICELLO

ADDRESS: 125 W. Broadway St., Monticello, Indiana 47960

ARTIST: Marguerite Zorach

TITLE: *Hay Making*

MEDIUM: Oil on canvas (mural)

STATUS: The Monticello post office is still an active, operating facility, and the mural can be viewed by interested members of the public. It resides in the lobby on the wall above the postmaster's door.

WEB: www.postofficefans.com/monticello-indiana-post-office/

Nappanee

ADDRESS: 202 E. Market St., Nappanee, Indiana 46550

ARTIST: Grant Christian

TITLE: *Waiting for the Mail*

MEDIUM: Oil on canvas (mural)

STATUS: The Nappanee post office is still an active, operating facility, and the mural can be viewed by interested members of the public. It resides in the lobby on the wall above the postmaster's door.

WEB: www.postofficefans.com/nappanee-indiana-post-office/

NORTH MANCHESTER

ADDRESS: 202 E. 2nd St., North Manchester, Indiana 46962

ARTIST: Alan Tompkins

TITLE: *Indiana Farm—Sunday Afternoon*

MEDIUM: Oil on canvas (mural)

STATUS: The North Manchester post office is still an active, operating facility, and the mural can be viewed by interested members of the public. It resides in the lobby on the wall above the postmaster's door.

WEB: www.postofficefans.com/north-manchester-indiana-post-office/

PAOLI

ADDRESS: 202 N. Gospel St., Paoli, Indiana 47454

ARTIST: Tom Rost

TITLE: *Rural Mail Carrier*

MEDIUM: Oil on canvas (mural)

STATUS: The Paoli post office is still an active, operating facility, and the mural can be viewed by interested members of the public. It resides in the lobby on the wall above the postmaster's door.

WEB: www.postofficefans.com/paoli-indiana-post-office/

PENDLETON

ADDRESS: 137 W. State St., Pendleton, Indiana 46064

ARTIST: William Frederick Kaeser

TITLE: *Loggers*

MEDIUM: Oil on canvas (mural)

STATUS: The Pendleton post office is still an active, operating facility, and the mural can be viewed by interested members of the public. It resides in the lobby on the wall above the postmaster's door.

WEB: www.postofficefans.com/pendleton-indiana-post-office/

RENSSELAER

ADDRESS: 225 S. Van Rensselaer St., Rensselaer, Indiana 47978

ARTIST: John Edward Costigan

TITLE: *Receiving the Mail on the Farm*

MEDIUM: Oil on canvas (mural)

STATUS: The Rensselaer post office is still an active, operating facility, and the mural can be viewed by interested members of the public. It resides in the lobby on the wall above the postmaster's door.

WEB: www.postofficefans.com/rensselaer-indiana-post-office/

ROCKVILLE

ADDRESS: 102 N. Market St., Rockville, Indiana 47872

ARTIST: Milton Avery

TITLE: *Landscape*

MEDIUM: Oil on canvas (mural)

STATUS: The Rockville post office is still an active, operating facility. The mural can be viewed by interested members of the pubic. It resides in the lobby on the wall above the postmaster's door.

WEB: www.postofficefans.com/rockville-indiana-post-office/

SPENCER

ADDRESS: 30 S. Washington St., Spencer, Indiana 47460

ARTIST: Joseph Meert

TITLE: *Harvesting*

MEDIUM: Oil and tempera (mural)

STATUS: The Spencer post office is still an active, operating facility, and the mural can be viewed by interested members of the public. It resides in the lobby on the wall above the postmaster's door. The Spencer mural was the winner in the 48 States Mural Competition in 1939.

WEB: www.postofficefans.com/spencer-indiana-post-office/

TELL CITY

ADDRESS: 516 Main St., Tell City, Indiana 47586

ARTIST: Laci de Gerenday

TITLE: *The Noon Mail*

MEDIUM: Wood (relief)

STATUS: The former Tell City post office is no longer an active, operating postal facility. The relief was moved to the new post office building where it can be viewed by interested members of the public. It resides in the retail section of the lobby on a wall behind the retail counter.

WEB: www.postofficefans.com/tell-city-indiana-former-post-office/

TERRE HAUTE

ADDRESS: 30 N. 7th St., Terre Haute, Indiana 47809

ARTIST: Frederick Well Ross

TITLE: *The Signing of the Magna Carta*

MEDIUM: Oil on canvas (murals)

STATUS: The former Terre Haute post office is no longer an active, operating postal facility. However, the murals still reside in the building. Interested members of the public should contact the Indiana State University for hours and accessibility. They reside on the wall of a former courtroom.

WEB: www.postofficefans.com/terre-haute-indiana-former-post-office-courthouse/

TIPTON

ADDRESS: 203 E. Jefferson St., Tipton, Indiana 46072

ARTIST: Donald Magnus Mattison

TITLE: *Indiana Farming*

MEDIUM: Oil on canvas (mural)

STATUS: The Tipton post office is still an active, operating facility, and the mural can be viewed by interested members of the public. It resides in the lobby on the wall above the postmaster's door.

WEB: www.postofficefans.com/tipton-indiana-post-office/

Union City

Address: 102 W. Pearl St., Union City, Indiana 47390

Artist: Donald Magnus Mattison

Title: *Country Cousins*

Medium: Oil on canvas (mural)

Status: The Union City post office is still an active, operating facility, and the mural can be viewed by interested members of the public. It resides in the lobby on the wall above the postmaster's door.

Web: www.postofficefans.com/union-city-indiana-post-office/

Summary

I CREATED THIS BOOK as a reference for myself, as well as for those who are interested in these wonderful buildings and works of art. My goal is to provide you a valuable reference list of the buildings in Indiana that house murals. For more information about each one and to participate in the discussion of any of the buildings or art, please visit www.postofficefans.com.

This book contains all the post offices in Indiana that had art installed as a part of the New Deal. This book provides notes on the location, status and accessibility of the art. I've personally visited, photographed or verified the status of each mural. Please note this is not a complete list of all the post office buildings constructed in Indiana during the New Deal, only the ones that housed art.

It is also worth noting that some of the images contained in this book were enhanced for production and your viewing pleasure. All photographs taken and edited by David W. Gates Jr.

I welcome your comments, suggestions, or feedback. You may reach me through the following social channels. Of course, I also welcome mail through the United States Postal Service. C/O Post Office Fans, PO Box 11, Crystal Lake, IL 60039.

ABOUT THE AUTHOR

DAVID W. GATES JR. is a post office enthusiast and award-winning
author who has traveled thousands
of miles nationwide in search of
historic post office buildings and
art. He blogs about his work at:

www.postofficefans.com

Although the murals have been
around for more than 88 years,
David discovered how often these
are overlooked. Join David in his
quest to visit them all.

He lives in Crystal Lake, Illinois
with his wife, son, and two cats. When not photographing and docu-
menting post offices, he can be found cooking, baking, hiking, or in-
volved in do-it-yourself projects at home, not necessarily all at once and
not necessarily in that order. To learn more about Mr. Gates and his
work please visit www.davidwgatesjr.net.

OTHER TITLES BY THE PUBLISHER

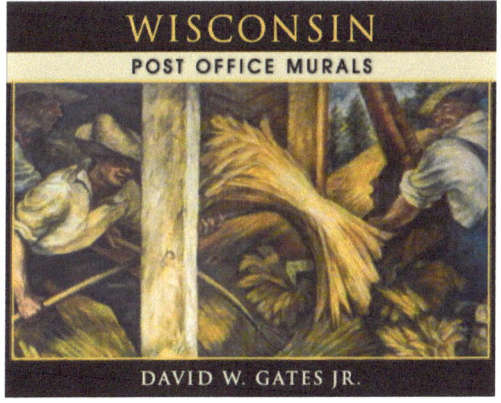

WISCONSIN POST OFFICE MURALS

by David W. Gates Jr.

ISBN: 978-1-970088-00-7 (Paperback)
ISBN: 978-1-970088-01-4 (EPUB)
ISBN: 978-1-970088-02-1 (PDF)

WISCONSIN POST OFFICE MURAL GUIDEBOOK

by David W. Gates Jr.

ISBN: 978-1-970088-09-0 (Paperback)
ISBN: 978-1-970088-10-6 (EPUB)
ISBN: 978-1-970088-11-3 (PDF)

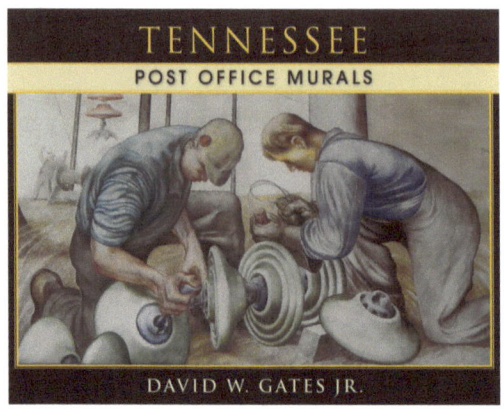

Tennessee Post Office Murals

by David W. Gates Jr.

ISBN: 978-1-970088-03-8 (Paperback)
ISBN: 978-1-970088-04-5 (EPUB)
ISBN: 978-1-970088-05-2 (PDF)

Tennessee Post Office Mural Guidebook

by David W. Gates Jr.

ISBN: 978-1-970088-0-69 (Paperback)
ISBN: 978-1-970088-0-76 (EPUB)
ISBN: 978-1-970088-0-83 (PDF)

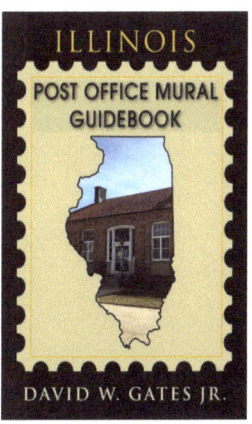

ILLINOIS POST OFFICE MURAL GUIDEBOOK

by David W. Gates Jr.

ISBN: 978-1-970088-12-0 (Paperback)
ISBN: 978-1-970088-13-7 (EPUB)
ISBN: 978-1-970088-14-4 (PDF)

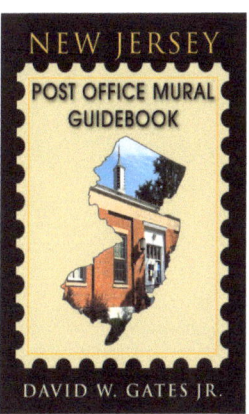

NEW JERSEY POST OFFICE MURAL GUIDEBOOK

by David W. Gates Jr.

ISBN: 978-1-970088-15-1 (Paperback)
ISBN: 978-1-970088-16-8 (EPUB)
ISBN: 978-1-970088-17-5 (PDF)

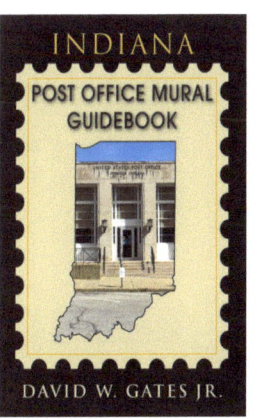

INDIANA POST OFFICE MURAL GUIDEBOOK

by David W. Gates Jr.

ISBN: 978-1-970088-18-2 (Paperback)
ISBN: 978-1-970088-19-9 (EPUB)
ISBN: 978-1-970088-20-5 (PDF